The World's Funniest Laws

JAMES ALEXANDER

In Arizona you can go to prison for 25 years for cutting down a cactus!

Do not say "oh boy" in Jonesborough, Georgia. It's illegal!

On Sundays in Florida, widows must not go parachuting!

It is against the law to take a lion to the cinema in Baltimore!

CJ

Crombie Jardine
PUBLISHING LIMITED

13 Nonsuch Walk, Cheam, Surrey, SM2 7LG
www.crombiejardine.com

This edition was first published by
Crombie Jardine Publishing Limited in 2005.

Copyright © 2005,
Crombie Jardine Publishing Limited.

ISBN: 1-905102-10-0

Compiled by James Alexander
Designed by 'Mr Stiffy'
Cartoons by Helen West
Printed and bound in the United Kingdom by
William Clowes Ltd, Beccles, Suffolk

CONTENTS PAGE

Where there are too many policemen,
there is no liberty.
Where there are too many soldiers,
there is no peace.
Where there are too many lawyers,
there is no justice.

Lin Yutang, Chinese-American Philosopher

INTRODUCTION

When we think of laws in the UK we recall the Magna Carta of about 800 years ago. All over Europe laws were formed and had time to mature over the centuries. Not so in the USA, which grew to be a world power in a relatively short period. Laws would spring up wherever people would settle. Any educated man could become a lawyer and any local judge could pass laws in his town that he felt appropriate.

In Waterloo, Nebraska, for example, barbers were forbidden to eat onions between the hours of 7am and 7pm. This must have been because a judge had an onion-eating, foul-breathed barber attend to him one day. What better way to avoid this in future than to pass a law? Hey presto! Problem solved.

Although most of these laws seem very silly to us now, at the time they must have been passed for a reason.

The section on funny American laws, which takes up most of the book, is divided alphabetically by State. It is an eclectic set of laws chosen by me for their weirdness and comic aspects. Each State's motto is noted after the State heading. A random collection of funny laws from other parts of the world follow but really, as you will see, America has the crown!

I hope you enjoy the book and if you have any comments you can direct them to me at my publisher: james@crombiejardine.com.

James Alexander
London 2005

"The first thing we'll do, let's kill all the lawyers."
William Shakespeare

AMERICA

ALABAMA

'UNFORGETTABLE'
State capital: Montgomery.
Became a State: 14 December 1819.

✪ It is unlawful to play dominoes on Sunday.

✪ It is illegal to wear a fake moustache that causes people to laugh in church.

✪ It is legal to drive the wrong way down a one-way street only if you have a lantern attached to the front of your car.

✪ Putting salt on a railroad track may be punishable by death.

✪ Loud talking is forbidden in Prichard.

**Never point a loaded snake at
someone - it could land you in jail.**

Alabama

ALASKA

'NORTH! TO ALASKA'
State Capital: Juneau.
Became a State: 3 January 1959.

- ✪ It is against the law to look at a moose from an airplane.

- ✪ It is also unlawful to push a live moose out of a moving airplane.

- ✪ It is legal to shoot bears, but forbidden to wake a sleeping bear for the purpose of taking a photograph of it.

- ✪ In Anchorage every year all male residents should, by law, grow beards from the 5th of January to the middle of February, when a celebration called the Fur Rendezvous is held.

- ✪ In Fairbanks it is illegal to give alcoholic drinks to a moose.

ARIZONA

'GRAND CANYON STATE'
State Capital: Phoenix.
Became a State: 14 February 1912.

✪ Donkeys are forbidden from
sleeping in bathtubs.

✪ It is unlawful to refuse a
person a glass of water.

✪ When being attacked by a criminal
or a burglar, you may only protect
yourself with the same weapon that
the other person possesses.

✪ In Tucson it is unlawful for
women to wear trousers.

✪ In Glendale it is illegal to
drive a car in reverse.

✪ In Globe it is against the law to play cards
in the street with a Native American.

○ Anyone caught stealing soap in Mohave Country can be made to wash with it until it is all used up.

○ It is illegal to wear suspenders in Nogales.

○ Cowboys in Phoenix cannot walk through hotel lobbies wearing spurs.

COURTROOM BLUNDERS

Lawyer: Do you recall approximately the time that you examined that body at the hospital?

Witness: It was in the evening. The autopsy started at about 5:30 pm.

Lawyer: And the person was dead at the time, is that correct?

Witness: No, you idiot! He was sitting on the table wondering why I was performing an autopsy on him!

COURTROOM BLUNDERS

Lawyer: Have you ever heard of Sigmund Freud?
Juror: Yes.
Lawyer: What have you heard?
Juror: He's in Las Vegas.
By the Court: I think you're thinking of Siegfried & Roy, aren't you?
Juror: That's what I'm doing.
Lawyer: This guy was a little older than that.

ARKANSAS

'THE NATURAL STATE'
State Capital: Little Rock.
Became a State: 15 June 1836.

- ✪ It is illegal for a man to beat his wife more than once a month.

- ✪ Schoolteachers who bob their hair may be forfeiting their pay rises.

- ✪ It is against the law for the Arkansas River to rise higher than to the Main Street bridge in Little Rock.

- ✪ In Fayetteville it is illegal to kill 'any living creature'.

CALIFORNIA

'FIND YOURSELF HERE'

State Capital: Sacramento.
Became a State: 9 September 1850.

✪ All animals are banned from mating in public within 1,500 feet of a bar, school, or place of worship.

✪ You are guilty of a misdemeanor if you shoot at any kind of game from a moving vehicle – unless, of course, the target is a whale. Then you're all right.

✪ It is unlawful to set a mousetrap unless you have a hunting licence.

✪ It is illegal to drive more than 2,000 sheep down Hollywood Boulevard at any one time.

✪ No vehicle without a driver may exceed 60 miles per hour.

- ✪ You can't sell snakes on the streets in California.

- ✪ It is against the law to cry on the witness stand in Los Angeles courts.

- ✪ In Long Beach it is forbidden to swear on a mini-golf course.

- ✪ In Pacific Grove you can be fined $500 for 'molesting' butterflies.

- ✪ In San Francisco it is unlawful to walk an elephant down Market Street without a leash.

- ✪ A 1929 law makes it illegal in Stockton to wiggle while dancing.

*Lawyers are always more ready to get a
man into troubles than out of them.*
William Goldsmith

*Lawyers are men whom we hire
to protect us from lawyers.*
Elbert Hubbard

 John was a miserly old lawyer who had
been diagnosed with a incurable illness.
He was determined to prove the saying,
'You can't take it with you,' was rubbish.

After much consideration, John worked out
how to take at least some of his money
with him when he died. He instructed
his wife to go to the bank and withdraw
enough money to fill two pillow cases.

He then directed her to take the bags of money to the attic and leave them directly above his bed. John's plan: when he died, he would reach out and grab the bags on his way to heaven.

Several weeks after the funeral, John's wife was up in the attic packing some things away, when she came across the two pillow cases stuffed with cash.

"Bloody fool!" she said out loud. "I knew he should have had me put the money in the cellar."

 An anxious woman went to her doctor.

"Doctor," she asked nervously, "Can you get pregnant from anal intercourse?"

"Of course," he replied, "Where do you think lawyers come from?"

COLORADO

'COLOURFUL COLORADO'

State Capital: Denver.
Became a State: 1 August 1876.

✪ In Logan County it is unlawful for a man to kiss a woman while she is asleep.

✪ In Pueblo it is illegal to let a dandelion grow within the city limits.

Have you heard about the lawyers word processor?
Whichever font you select, everything comes out in fine print.

What's the difference between a lawyer and a vulture?
Vultures wait until you're dead to rip your heart out.

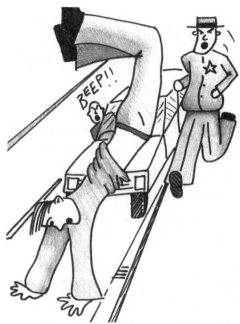

**In Hartford it is illegal to cross the
street while walking on your hands.**

Connecticut

CONNECTICUT

'WE'RE FULL OF SURPRISES'
State Capital: Hartford.
Became a State: 9 January 1788.

✪ By law, in order for a pickle to be officially considered a pickle, it must bounce.

✪ It is unlawful to dispose of used razor blades.

✪ You risk a $5.00 fine by carrying a corpse in a taxi in Hartford.

✪ In New Britain the speed limit for fire trucks is 25 mph, even when going to a fire.

In Hartford, it is unlawful to educate a dog.

Connecticut

A Rabbi, a Hindu, and a lawyer are in a car together. They run out of petrol and are forced to stop at a farmer's house. As there are only two spare beds, the farmer says that unfortunately one of the men will have to sleep in the barn.

The Hindu says, "I'm humble, I will sleep in the barn," and goes out to the barn. In a few minutes, the farmer hears a knock at the door. It's the Hindu and he says, "There is a cow in the barn. It's against my religion to sleep with a cow."

So, the Rabbi says, "I'm humble, I'll sleep in the barn," and goes to the barn. A few minutes later, the farmer hears a knock at the door. It's the Rabbi and he says, "I'm sorry but it is against my religion to sleep where there is a pig and there is a pig in the barn."

So the lawyer is forced to go and sleep in the barn. A few minutes later, there is a knock at the door.

It's the pig and the cow...

 How do you save five drowning lawyers?
Who cares?

DELAWARE

'THE FIRST STATE'
State Capital: Dover.
Became a State: 7 December 1787.

✪ Getting married on a dare is grounds for an annulment.

✪ It is illegal to pawn your wooden leg in Delaware.

✪ It is unlawful to fly over any body of water, unless you are carrying ample supplies of food and drink with you.

✪ In Sarasota it is illegal to sing while you are wearing a swimsuit.

**Unmarried women who parachute
on Sundays may be jailed.**

Delaware

FLORIDA

'SUNSHINE STATE'
State Capital: Tallahassee.
Became a State: 3 March 1845.

- If you tie an elephant to a parking meter, you must pay the parking fee just as you would for a vehicle.

- It is against the law to sing in a public place while wearing a swimsuit.

- You are breaking the law if you skateboard without a licence.

- Women may be fined for falling asleep under a hair dryer, as can the salon owner.

- Having sexual relations with a porcupine is definitely not legal.

- Men may not be seen publicly in any kind of strapless gown.

✪ Oral sex is illegal.

✪ The penalty for horse theft is death by hanging.

✪ When having sex, only the missionary position is legal.

✪ You are not allowed to break more than three dishes per day, or chip the edges of more than four cups and/or saucers.

✪ You may not fart in a public place after 6pm on Thursdays.

✪ You may not kiss your wife's breasts.

What do you call a block of cement containing ten lawyers?
A waste of cement.

COURTROOM BLUNDERS

Lawyer: Do you know if your daughter has ever been involved in Voodoo or the occult?
Witness: We both do.
Lawyer: Voodoo?
Witness: We do.
Lawyer: You do?
Witness: Yes. Voodoo.

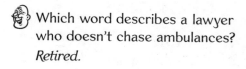 Which word describes a lawyer
who doesn't chase ambulances?
Retired.

Why is it that many lawyers
have broken noses?
From chasing parked ambulances.

What happens when a lawyer takes Viagra?
He gets taller.

GEORGIA

'GEORGIA ON MY MIND'

State Capital: Atlanta.
Became a State: 2 January 1788.

○ It is considered a misdemeanor
for anyone to attend church on
Sundays without a loaded rifle.

○ It is only legal to change the
clothes on a shop front mannequin
when the blinds are down.

○ No one may carry an ice cream cone
in their back pocket on Sundays.

○ It is illegal for a chicken to
cross a road in Quitman.

In Atlanta it is illegal to tie a giraffe to a telephone pole or a street lamp.

Georgia

HAWAII

'THE ISLANDS OF ALOHA'
State Capital: Honolulu.
Became a State: 21 August 1959.

✪ **It is against the law to appear in public wearing only swimming trunks.**

✪ **It is illegal to own a mongoose without a permit.**

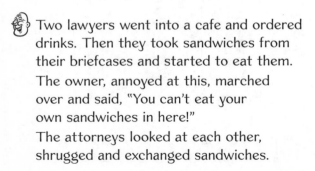

Two lawyers went into a cafe and ordered drinks. Then they took sandwiches from their briefcases and started to eat them.

The owner, annoyed at this, marched over and said, "You can't eat your own sandwiches in here!"

The attorneys looked at each other, shrugged and exchanged sandwiches.

COURTROOM BLUNDERS

Lawyer: Officer, when you stopped the defendant, were your red and blue lights flashing?
Witness: Yes.
Lawyer: Did the defendant say anything to you when she got out of her car?
Witness: Yes sir.
Lawyer: What did she say to you?
Witness: She said, "What disco am I at?"

 God decided to take the devil to court in order to settle their differences once and for all.

When Satan heard this, he laughed and said, "And where do you think you're going to find a lawyer?"

IDAHO

'DISCOVER IDAHO'
State Capital: Boise.
Became a State: 3 July 1890.

✪ Boxes of candy given as romantic gifts must weigh more than 50 pounds.

✪ It is against the law for people living in Idaho to participate in dog fights.

✪ In Pocatello, 'It is prohibited for pedestrians and motorists to display frowns, grimaces, scowls, threatening and glowering looks, gloomy and depressed facial appearances, generally all of which reflect unfavorably upon the city's reputation.'

✪ It is unlawful for anyone to sleep in a dog kennel in Wallace.

**It is against the law to go fishing
while sitting on a camel.**

Idaho

ILLINOIS

'A MILLION MILES FROM MONDAY'
State Capital: Springfield.
Became a State: 3 December 1818.

✿ You may be arrested for vagrancy
if you do not have at least one
dollar bill on your person.

✿ In Chicago it is against the law
to fish in your pyjamas.

✿ Also in Chicago, it is illegal to take
a French poodle to the opera.

✿ In Gurnee if you are a woman weighing more
than 200 pounds you are forbidden from
wearing shorts when you go horse riding.

✿ Women in Joliet can be jailed for trying on
more than six dresses in any one shop.

✿ Also in Joliet, it is against the law to
mispronounce the name Joliet.

**In Chicago it is against the law to
eat in a place that is on fire.**

Illinois

A lawyer was standing in a long line to get tickets for a play. Suddenly, he felt the hands of the man behind him, kneading into his back. He turned and gave the man a stern look, and the kneading stopped. But a few minutes later, he again felt the man's hands on his back.

"Excuse me," the lawyer asked, "but why are you touching my back?"

"I'm a chiropractor," the man replied, "and sometimes I can't help myself."

"Well get a grip, man!" the lawyer shot back. "I'm a lawyer, and you don't see me screwing the guy in front of me, do you?"

- ✪ In Kirkland it is illegal for bees to fly over the village or through any of its streets.

- ✪ In Macomb it is unlawful for a car to impersonate a wolf.

- ✪ It is against the law to make faces at dogs in Normal.

- ✪ In Oak Park it is against the law to fry more than a hundred doughnuts in a single day.

- ✪ A Zeigler law states that only the first four firemen reaching a fire will be paid for their services.

**In Zion it is illegal to give a
cat or dog a cigar.**

Illinois

INDIANA

'THE WELCOME MATS ALWAYS OUT'

State Capital: Indianapolis.
Became a State: 11 December 1816.

✪ Cheque forgery is punishable with a public flogging of up to 100 lashes.

✪ It is against the law for a man to be sexually aroused in public.

✪ It is against the law for any liquour store to sell milk.

✪ Moustaches are illegal if the bearer has a tendency to regularly kiss other humans.

✪ You can get out of paying for a dependent's medical care by praying for him/her.

✪ In Gary it is illegal to attend the theatre within four hours of eating garlic.

○ In Hammond if you stand still and look lazy you can legally be classified as a loiterer.

○ Monkeys are forbidden to smoke cigarettes in South Bend.

○ 'The Stepford Wives' is banned in Warsaw.

What's the worst part about seeing five lawyers in Cadillac go over a cliff?
A Cadillac seats six.

What can a goose do, a duck can't, and a lawyer should?
Stick his bill up his backside.

In Illinois your pet animal can be
sent to jail. A monkey spent five
days in jail for smoking!

Illinois

What do you get when you cross
the Godfather with a lawyer?
An offer you can't understand.

What is a criminal lawyer?
Redundant.

What does a lawyer use for contraception?
His personality.

What happens when you cross
a pig with a lawyer?
*Nothing. There are some things
even a pig won't do.*

How many lawyers does it take to stop
a cement truck travelling at 60 mph?
Never enough.

IOWA

'COME BE OUR GUEST'
State Capital: Des Moines.
Became a State: 28 December 1846.

- ✪ Iowa law makes it illegal to have a rotten egg in your possession.

- ✪ All establishments are forbidden to charge admission to see a one-armed piano player.

- ✪ Firemen in Fort Madison are required to practise for 15 minutes before attending a fire.

- ✪ Horses are forbidden from eating fire hydrants in Marshalltown.

**In Iowa it is illegal to leave an
aircraft whilst in flight.**

Iowa

KANSAS

'HEART OF AMERICA'S WEST'
State Capital: Topeka.
Became a State: 29 January 1861.

✪ It is against the law in this State
to eat snakes on a Sunday.

✪ In Garden City the law says you can't
drink from the public drinking fountains.

✪ In Kansas City if you are a minor you
cannot by law buy a cap gun, but you
can, on the other hand, buy a shotgun.

✪ In Lang it is against the law to
ride a mule down Main Street in
August, unless, of course, the said
mule is wearing a straw hat.

✪ You can't carry bees around in your
hat on the city streets in Lawrence.

✪ In Natoma it is illegal to throw a knife
at anyone wearing a striped shirt.
[However tempting it may be.]

✪ In Topeka it is against the
law to annoy squirrels.

✪ In Wichita a man's mistreatment
of his mother-in-law may not be
used as grounds for divorce.

✪ It is illegal to carry a concealed
bean snapper in Wichita.

✪ Also in Wichita, no father can frighten
his daughter's boyfriend with a gun.

A minister and a lawyer were chatting at a party:

"What do you do if you realize you've made a mistake on a case?" the minister asked.

"I try to fix it if it's a big one and ignore it if it's insignificant," replied the lawyer. "What do you do?"

The minister replied innocently, "Oh, more or less the same. For example, the other day I meant to say 'the devil is the father of liars,' but instead I said 'the devil is the father of lawyers,' so I let it go."

COURTROOM BLUNDERS

Lawyer: Remember all your responses must be oral. OK? Now, what school do you go to?
Witness: Oral.
Lawyer: How old are you?
Witness: Oral.

Lawyer: Did you ever stay all night with this man in Scunthorpe?
Witness: I refuse to answer that question.
Lawyer: Did you ever stay all night with this man in Goole?
Witness: I refuse to answer that question.
Lawyer: Did you ever stay all night with this man in Hull?
Witness: No.

In Kentucky you can be arrested for not bathing at least once a year.

Kentucky

KENTUCKY

'ALWAYS IN SEASON'

State Capital: Frankfurt.
Became a State: 1 June 1792.

✪ A person can be sent to jail for five years for merely sending a bottle of beer, wine or spirits as a gift to a friend in Kentucky.

✪ It is against the law to remarry the same man four times.

✪ In Kentucky you could be up on charges of contributory negligence for being behind a mule without first speaking to the animal.

✪ Legally you are deemed sober unless 'you cannot hold onto the ground.'

COURTROOM BLUNDERS

Lawyer: What is your date of birth, sir?
Witness: July 17th.
Lawyer: What year?
Witness: Every year.

Lawyer: Then there's a minus $85,000 plus interest. What did you believe that referenced when you signed it?
Witness: Creative financing.
Lawyer: But seriously folks!

LOUISIANA

'COME AS YOU ARE, LEAVE DIFFERENT'

State Capital: Baton Rouge.
Became a State: 30 April 1812.

✪ Forget gargling in public – it is against the law in this State.

✪ Be warned – you could land in jail for up to a year for making a false promise.

✪ In New Orleans fire trucks are required by law to stop at all red lights.

✪ Also in New Orleans, it is considered 'simple assault' to bite someone; and if the biter has false teeth, then it is 'aggravated assault'.

**It is illegal to rob a bank and then shoot
at the bank teller with a water pistol.**

Louisiana

MAINE

'MAINE IS ON THE MOVE'

State Capital: Augusta.
Became a State: 15 March 1820.

✪ The most money one can legally
win by gambling is $3.00.

✪ If you are a tenant in Rumford it is
illegal for you to bite your landlord.

✪ In Waterville it is against the law
to blow your nose in public.

What do you get when you cross
a librarian with a lawyer?
*All the information you need - but you
can't understand a word of it.*

A lawyer, a priest, and a young boy are in a plane about to crash and there are only two parachutes.

The lawyer says that since he is the smartest man on the plane, he deserves to survive. He takes a chute and jumps.

The priest looks at the young boy and tells him to take the last parachute since he has already lived a wonderful and full life.

The boy replies, "You can have the other chute, mister, because the smartest man on the plane just jumped with my book bag!"

In Portland it is against the law
for men to tickle women under
the chin with feather dusters.

Maine

MARYLAND

'SO MANY THINGS TO DO SO CLOSE TOGETHER'

State Capital: Annapolis.
Became a State: 28 April 1788.

✪ Every person who has bowled since 1833 may be fined $2 for each offence.

✪ It is illegal to mistreat oysters.

✪ It is against the law to play Randy Newman's 'Short People' on the radio.

✪ In Baltimore it is illegal to wash or scrub sinks, no matter how dirty they get.

✪ It is against the law in Halethorpe to kiss for more than one second.

Lions may not be taken to the theatre in Maryland.

Maryland

MASSACHUSETTS

'WE'D LOVE TO SHOW YOU AROUND'

State Capital: Boston.
Became a State: 6 February 1788.

✪ In 1659 Christmas was outlawed in this State.

✪ If you want to wear a goatee be sure you have a licence; you will be breaking the law without it.

✪ State legislation forbids duelling with water pistols.

✪ Be prepared: it is unlawful to deliver nappies on Sundays, whatever the emergency.

✪ Peanuts may not be eaten in court.

✪ In Boston it is against the law to take a bath unless you have been ordered to do so by a physician.

✪ In Holyoke it is unlawful to water your lawn when it is raining.

✪ North Andover citizens are forbidden to carry 'space guns'.

✪ If you live in Southbridge you had better not read books or newspapers after 8pm in the streets; it is against the law.

MICHIGAN

'GREAT THINGS TO SEE AND DO'

State Capital: Lansing.
Became a State: 26 January 1837.

- ✪ In Michigan a woman's hair legally belongs to her husband.

- ✪ Michigan law insists that dentists are officially classified as 'mechanics'.

- ✪ In Detroit you can only make love in a car if it is parked on your property.

- ✪ In Grand Rapids you face a fine if you are caught 'embracing or being embraced while a car is in motion'.

- ✪ In Port Huron the speed limit for ambulances in 20 mph.

MINNESOTA

'EXPLORE MINNESOTA'

State Capital: Saint Paul.
Became a State: 11 May 1858.

✪ Double-parkers can be put on a chain gang.

✪ It is against the law to tease skunks.

✪ Women impersonating Santa Claus
may face up to 30 days in jail.

✪ Every man in Brainerd is required
by law to grow a beard.

✪ Cats in International Falls are not allowed
to chase dogs up telephone poles.

In Minnesota it is illegal to cross the State line with a duck on your head.

Minnesota

*Anybody who thinks talk is cheap
should get some legal advice.*
Franklin P. Jones

*Ignorance of the law excuses no
man - from practising it.*
Adison Mizner

 What do you get if you beat
the shit out of a lawyer?
An empty suit.

MISSISSIPPI

'THE SOUTH'S WARMEST WELCOME'

State Capital: Jackson.
Became a State: 10 December 1817.

○ It is still legal to kill your servant.

○ It is against the law to teach others what polygamy is.

○ In Jackson if you want to burn down your house you must first remove the roof.

○ A would-be groom in Truro must 'prove himself manly' before marriage by hunting and killing either six blackbirds or three crows.

COURTROOM BLUNDERS

Lawyer: But if the discount wasn't on the sales order form or the invoice or the monthly printout, where would it be?
Witness: In Kansas, along with Dorothy and Toto.

Lawyer: So, you are unconscious, and they pulled you from the lake. What happened then?
Witness: Mr. Stewart gave me artificial insemination, you know, mouth-to-mouth.

MISSOURI

'SHOW ME MISSOURI'
State Capital: Jefferson City.
Became a State: 10 August 1821.

✪ Anyone under 21 years of age who takes out the household rubbish containing even a single empty alcoholic drink's container can be charged with illegal possession of alcohol.

✪ Drunkenness is deemed an 'inalienable right'.

✪ Children in Kansas City cannot by law buy toy cap guns. But they can buy shotguns if they want.

✪ In Saco women are forbidden from wearing hats that 'might frighten timid persons, children or animals'.

**Never let a sheep be in the cab of
your lorry without a chaperone
as it will get you jail time.**

Montana

MONTANA

'BIG SKY COUNTRY'
State Capital: Helena.
Became a State: 8 November 1889.

✪ It is a criminal act for a wife to open her husband's mail.

✪ It is a misdemeanor to show movies that depict acts of felonious crime.

✪ In Whitehall it is against the law to operate a vehicle with ice picks attached to the wheels.

Why are lawyers buried a full
20 feet in the ground?
Because deep down they're great people.

 A woman and her little girl were visiting
the grave of the little girl's grandmother.

On their way back to the car, the little
girl asked, "Mummy, do they ever bury
two people in the same grave?"

"No, sweetheart," replied the
mother. "Why do you ask?"

"The tombstone back there said, 'Here
lies a lawyer and an honest man.'"

NEBRASKA

'GENUINE'

State Capital: Lincoln.
Became a State: 1 March 1867.

- ✪ It is illegal for a mother to give her daughter a perm without a licence.

- ✪ It is against the law for bar owners to sell beer unless they are simultaneously brewing a kettle of soup.

- ✪ In Nebraska it is forbidden to picnic twice on the same spot within any 30-day period.

- ✪ Barbers in Omaha are forbidden from shaving their customers' chests.

- ✪ Parents in Omaha be warned: if your child burps during a church service you may be arrested.

- ✪ In Waterloo barbers are forbidden from eating onions between 7am and 7pm.

COURTROOM BLUNDERS

Prosecutor: Did you kill the victim?
Defendant: No, I did not.
Prosecutor: Do you know what the penalties are for perjury?
Defendant: Yes, I do. And they're a hell of a lot better than the penalty for murder.

NEVADA

'DISCOVER BOTH SIDES OF NEVADA'

State Capital: Carson City.
Became a State: 31 October 1864.

- ✪ It is forbidden to drive a camel on the highway.

- ✪ It is still 'legal' to hang someone for shooting your dog on your property.

- ✪ Everyone walking on the streets of Elko is required to wear a mask.

- ✪ Men who wear moustaches in Eureka are forbidden from kissing women.

- ✪ In Nyala a man is forbidden from buying drinks for more than three people other than himself at any one period during the day.

COURTROOM BLUNDERS

Lawyer: Doctor, did you say he
was shot in the woods?
Witness: No. I said he was shot
in the lumbar region.

Lawyer: Are you married?
Witness: No. I'm divorced.
Lawyer: And what did your husband
do before you divorced him?
Witness: A lot of things I didn't know about.

Lawyer: Doctor, as a result of
your examination of the plaintiff,
is the young lady pregnant?
Witness: The young lady is pregnant,
but not as a result of my examination.

NEW HAMPSHIRE

'THE ROAD LESS TRAVELLED'
State Capital: Concord.
Became a State: 21 June 1788.

✪ It is illegal to sell the clothes you are
wearing to pay off a gambling debt.

✪ It is forbidden to check into a
hotel under an assumed name.

✪ New Hampshire law forbids you
to tap your foot, nod your head,
or in any way keep time to music
in a bar, restaurant, or cafe.

✪ On Sundays citizens may not relieve
themselves while looking up.

NEW JERSEY

'NEW JERSEY AND YOU ARE PERFECT TOGETHER'

State Capital: Trenton.
Became a State: 18 December 1787.

✪ It is forbidden to frown at a police officer.

✪ It is against the law for a
person to slurp soup.

✪ It is against the law for pigeons
to fly over Bayonne, New Jersey,
unless they are licensed.

✪ In Newark it is against the law to sell
ice cream after 6pm, unless customers
have notes from their doctors.

✪ In Trenton it is unlawful to throw
a bad pickle in the street.

COURTROOM BLUNDERS

By the Court: Is there any reason why you couldn't serve as a juror in this case?
Potential Juror: I don't want to be away from my job that long.
The Court: Can't they do without you at work?
Juror: Yes, but I don't want them to know that.

NEW MEXICO

'LAND OF ENCHANTMENT'

State capital: Santa Fe.
Became a State: 6 January 1912.

✪ The Merriam–Webster Collegiate
Dictionary is banned in Carlsbad.

✪ In Raton if you are a woman it is illegal
for you to ride horseback down a
public street wearing a kimono.

What do you call a lawyer at
the bottom of the sea?
A start.

What do you call all the lawyers in the
world at the bottom of the sea?
A result.

COURTROOM BLUNDERS

Lawyer: What gear were you in
at the moment of impact?
Witness: Burberry sweatshirt and trainers.

Lawyer: Can you describe the individual?

Witness: He was about medium
height and had a beard.

Lawyer: Was this a male or a female?

Lawyer: Was that the same
nose you broke as a child?

NEW YORK

'I LOVE NEW YORK'
State Capital: Albany.
Became a State: 27 July 1788.

- ✪ The penalty for jumping off a building is death.

- ✪ New York has a law forbidding blind men from driving automobiles.

- ✪ In New York City, 'It is disorderly conduct for one man to greet another on the street by placing the end of his thumb against the tip of his nose, at the same time extending and wiggling the fingers of his hand.'

- ✪ If you are Santa Claus in New York City, by law you must make sure that the whiskers you wear in public are fireproof.

- ✪ To lay a hose on the lawn or to use a sprinkler for watering your lawn is unlawful in Staten Island, New York.

A defendant was asked if he wanted a bench trial or a jury trial.

"Jury trial," the defendant replied.

"Do you understand the difference?" asked the judge.

"Sure," replied the defendant. "That's where twelve ignorant people decide my fate instead of one."

 A physician, an engineer and a lawyer were arguing about whose profession was the oldest.

The surgeon announced, "Remember how God removed a rib from Adam to create Eve? Obviously, medicine is the oldest profession."

The engineer replied, "But before that,

God created the heavens and the earth from chaos, in less than a week. You have to admit that was a remarkable feat of engineering, and that makes engineering an older profession than medicine."

The lawyer smirked, and merely enquired, "And who do you think created the chaos?"

NORTH CAROLINA

'A BETTER PLACE TO BE'
State Capital: Raleigh.
Became a State: 21 November 1789.

✪ In Asheville it is illegal to
sneeze on city streets.

✪ In Charlotte women must have
their bodies covered by at least
16 yards of cloth at all times.

Did you hear about the terrorists who took
a whole courtroom full of lawyers hostage?
*They threatened to release one every
hour until their demands where met.*

NORTH DAKOTA

'DISCOVER THE SPIRIT'
State Capital: Bismark.
Became a State: 2 November 1889.

- ✪ It is illegal to lie down and fall asleep with your shoes on.

- ✪ It is against the law to serve beer and pretzels at the same time in any bar, club, or restaurant in this State.

- ✪ If you happen to meet a man in North Dakota who is wanted for a felony and he refuses to go with you to a police station, you are legally entitled to shoot him!

- ✪ In Fargo you can be jailed for wearing a hat while dancing, or even for wearing a hat to a function where dancing is taking place.

COURTROOM BLUNDERS

Lawyer: Do you believe you are
emotionally stable?
Witness: I used to be.
Lawyer: How many times have
you committed suicide?

Lawyer: So, you were gone until you returned?

Lawyer: You say that the stairs
went down to the basement?
Witness: Yes.
Lawyer: And these stairs, did they go up also?

OHIO

'HEART OF IT ALL'

State Capital: Columbus.
Became a State: 1 March 1803.

○ In Columbus it is against the law for shops to sell corn flakes on a Sunday.

○ 'Catch 22' is banned in Strongville.

○ In Youngstown, it is illegal to run out of petrol.

○ Also in Youngstown, it is against the law to ride on the roof on a taxi.

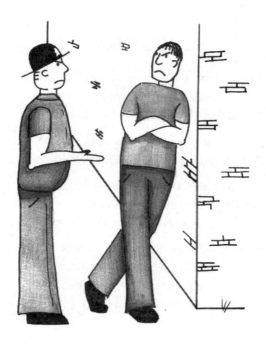

Clinton County calls for a fine for anyone caught leaning against a public building.

Ohio

OKLAHOMA

'NATIVE AMERICAN'
State Capital: Oklahoma City.
Became a State: 16 November 1907.

- ✪ People who make 'ugly faces' at dogs may be fined and/or jailed.

- ✪ It is against the law to wash clothing in a public drinking fountain or birdbath in Duncan.

- ✪ In Forgan it is illegal for you to ride your bicycle backwards on the main streets.

**It's against the law to get a
fish drunk in Oklahoma.**

Oklahoma

OREGON

'THINGS LOOK DIFFERENT HERE'

State Capital: Salem.
Became a State: 14 February 1859.

✪ In Oregan you are not allowed to bathe without wearing 'suitable clothing': that which covers the body from neck to knee.

✪ You are forbidden to allow a horse to ride around in the back seat of your car in Hillsboro.

✪ In Hood River it is prohibited to juggle without a licence.

✪ Marion ministers are forbidden from eating garlic or onions before delivering a sermon.

✪ Oregon law forbids the use of canned corn in fishing. [Canned corn does work – try it!]

✪ In Portland it is illegal to wear roller skates in public toilets.

✪ Also in Portland it is against the law to parade up and down the street with a 'For Sale' sign.

✪ Salem has barred women's wrestling.

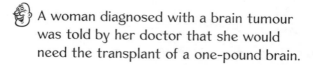 A woman diagnosed with a brain tumour was told by her doctor that she would need the transplant of a one-pound brain.

The doctor then asked, "What type of brain do you want?"

"What type?" the woman asked, confused.

"Yes," replied the doctor. "There is a substantial difference in price. For example, a one-pound brain of a surgeon costs £5,000, while you can get a one-pound brain of a nuclear physicist for £4,000, and so on.'

"Can you give me a one-pound lawyer's
brain? Ever since I was a little girl
I've dreamed of being a lawyer."

"That's pricey, though: £25,000,"
the doctor replied.

"Why so much?" the woman asked.
"That's over four times what
a surgeon's brain costs!"

"Do you have any idea how many
lawyers it takes to produce a pound
of brain?" the doctor replied.

PENNSYLVANIA

'MEMORIES LAST A LIFETIME'
State Capital: Harrisburg.
Became a State: 12 December 1787.

✪ 'Any motorist who sights a team of
horses coming toward him must pull

well off the road, cover his car with a blanket or canvas that blends with the countryside, and let the horses pass. If the horses appear skittish, the motorist must take his car apart, piece by piece, and hide it under the nearest bushes.'

✪ It is against the law to throw pickle juice on a trolley.

✪ Beards more than two and a half feet long are forbidden by law in Altoona.

✪ In Morrisville women need a permit to wear cosmetics.

✪ It is illegal to smoke a pipe after sunset in Newport.

✪ In Providence it is forbidden to sell toothpaste and a toothbrush to the same customer on a Sunday.

COURTROOM BLUNDERS

Lawyer: The youngest son, the 20-year-old, how old is he?

Lawyer: She had three children, right?
Witness: Yes.
Lawyer: How many were boys?
Witness: None.
Lawyer: Were there any girls?

RHODE ISLAND

'AND PROVIDENCE PLANTATIONS'

State Capital: Providence.
Became a State: 29 May 1790.

✪ **In Central Falls it is illegal to pour pickle juice on car tracks.**

 Two lawyers walking through the woods spotted a fierce-looking bear.

The first lawyer immediately opens his briefcase, pulls out a pair of Nikes and starts putting them on.

The second lawyer looks at him and says, "Are you mad? You'll never be able to outrun that bear!"

"I don't have to," the first lawyer replies. "I only have to outrun you."

COURTROOM BLUNDERS

Lawyer: Any suggestions as to what prevented this from being a murder trial instead of an attempted murder trial?
Witness: The victim lived.

Lawyer: What is the meaning of sperm being present?
Witness: It indicates intercourse.
Lawyer: Male sperm?
Witness: That's the only kind I know of.

Lawyer: When was the last time you saw the deceased?
Witness: At his funeral.
Lawyer: Did he make any comments to you at that time?

SOUTH CAROLINA

'SMILING FACES BEAUTIFUL PLACES'

State Capital: Columbia.
Became a State: 23 May 1788.

- ✪ Every citizen is obliged to carry his gun to church.

- ✪ In Anderson it is against the law for anyone to curl up on the railway lines and take a nap.

- ✪ In Charleston all carriage horses must wear nappies.

- ✪ No horses are allowed into Fountain Inn unless they are wearing pants.

COURTROOM BLUNDERS

Lawyer: Now, doctor, isn't it true that when a person dies in his sleep, in most cases, he just passes quietly away and doesn't know anything about it until the next morning?

Lawyer: And what happened then?
Witness: He told me, he says, "I have to kill you because you can identify me."
Lawyer: Did he kill you?

Lawyer: Was it you or your brother that was killed in the war?

SOUTH DAKOTA

'GREAT FACES GREAT PLACES'

State Capital: Pierre.
Became a State: 2 November 1889.

- ✪ It is illegal to lie down and fall asleep in a cheese factory.

- ✪ Movies that show police officers being struck, beaten, or treated in an offensive manner are forbidden.

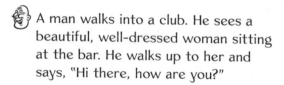 A man walks into a club. He sees a beautiful, well-dressed woman sitting at the bar. He walks up to her and says, "Hi there, how are you?"

She turns to him, looks him straight in the eyes and says, "I'll screw anybody any time, any where."

The guy raises his eyebrows
and says, "Really? And which law
firm do you work for?"

I broke a mirror the other day.
That's seven years bad luck, but my
lawyer thinks he can get me five.

Why does California have the most
lawyers in the country, and New Jersey
have the most toxic waste sites?
New Jersey got first choice.

TENNESSEE

'SOUNDS GOOD TO ME'

State Capital: Nashville.
Became a State: 1 June 1796.

✪ It is against the law to use a lasso to catch a fish.

✪ In Dyersburg it is illegal for a woman
to call a man for a date.

✪ In Memphis restaurants it is prohibited
to give any pie to fellow diners. It is also
illegal to take unfinished pie home. All
pie must be eaten on the premises.

✪ It is against the law for a woman to drive by
herself in Memphis; 'a man must walk or run in
front of the vehicle, waving a red flag in order to
warn approaching pedestrians and motorists.'

✪ Also in Memphis, frogs are prohibited
from croaking after 11pm.

In Texas it is illegal to put graffiti on someone else's cow.

Texas

TEXAS

'IT'S LIKE A WHOLE OTHER COUNTRY'

State Capital: Austin.
Became a State: 29 December 1845.

✪ A Texan anti-crime law requires criminals to give their victims 24 hours' notice, either orally or in writing, and to explain the nature of the crime to be committed.

✪ It is illegal to milk another person's cow.

✪ In Texas you are not allowed to take more than three sips of beer at a time while standing.

✪ The entire 'Encyclopedia Britannica' is banned in this State because it contains a formula for making beer at home.

✪ In Houston it is against the law to sell Limburger cheese on a Sunday.

✪ Also in Houston, beer may not be purchased after midnight on a Sunday, but can be purchased anytime on a Monday... Which happens to begin right after midnight on a Sunday! [So it's illegal to buy it when it's legal to buy it?]

✪ In Mesquite it is illegal for children to have unusual haircuts.

UTAH

'THE GREATEST SNOW ON EARTH'

State Capital: Salt Lake City.
Became a State: 4 January 1896.

✪ By law birds have the right of way on all highways here.

✪ A husband is responsible for every criminal act committed by his wife while she is in his presence.

✪ No one may have sex in the back of an ambulance if it is responding to an emergency call.

✪ Daylight must be visible between partners on a dance floor in Monroe.

✪ In Salt Lake City you cannot give away a fish on a Sunday or on a public holiday.

COURTROOM BLUNDERS

Lawyer: I show you Exhibit 3 and ask you if you recognize that picture?
Witness: That's me.
Lawyer: Were you present when that picture was taken?

Lawyer: Were you present in court this morning when you were sworn in?

VERMONT

'GREEN MOUNTAIN STATE'
State Capital: Montpelier.
Became a State: 4 March 1791.

✪ It is unlawful to deny the existence of God.

✪ It is against the law to whistle underwater.

✪ If you are a woman in Vermont and wish to wear false teeth, you must first get written permission to do so from your husband.

*It is better to be a mouse in a cat's mouth
than a man in a lawyer's hands.*
Spanish Proverb

COURTROOM BLUNDERS

Lawyer: What was the first thing your husband
said to you when he woke that morning?
Witness: He said, "Where am I Cheryl?"
Lawyer: And why did that upset you?
Witness: My name is Kathy.

VIRGINIA

'VIRGINIA IS FOR LOVERS'
State Capital: Richmond.
Became a State: 25 June 1788.

- ✪ Bathtubs are forbidden in the house; they must be kept in the garden.

- ✪ In Virginia it is illegal to handle snakes in church.

- ✪ There is a State law prohibiting 'corrupt practices of bribery by any person other than candidates'.

- ✪ In Lebanon it is against the law to kick your wife out of bed.

- ✪ In any eating establishment in Richmond it is against the law to flip a coin to determine who buys a cup of coffee.

- ✪ Only babies are allowed to ride in baby carriages in Roderfield.

WASHINGTON

'A LITTLE TRIP TO THE EXTRAORDINARY'

State Capital: Olympia.
Became a State: 11 November 1889.

✪ Don't pretend that your parents are rich when they are not – it's illegal here.

✪ Washington law says that a driver of a car not equipped with ashtrays is liable to a fine of $200.00.

✪ X-rays may not be used to fit shoes.

✪ Seattle residents may not carry concealed weapons longer than six feet.

COURTROOM BLUNDERS

Lawyer: And where was the location of the accident?
Witness: Approximately junction 23 on the M1.
Lawyer: And where is junction 23?
Witness: Probably between junction 22 and junction 24.

Lawyer: Sir, what is your IQ?
Witness: Well, I think I can see pretty well.

WEST VIRGINIA

'WILD AND WONDERFUL'

State Capital: Charleston.
Became a State: 20 June 1863.

⊙ A person may not persuade another to kill a frog for him in West Virginia.

⊙ It is illegal to snooze on a train.

⊙ Whistling underwater is prohibited.

⊙ In Nicholas County no clergy members may tell jokes or humorous stories from the pulpit during church services.

It is unfair to believe everything we hear about lawyers, some of it might not be true.
Gerald F. Lieberman

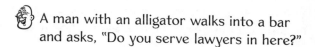 A man with an alligator walks into a bar and asks, "Do you serve lawyers in here?"

"We sure do!" replies the barman.

"Great!" says the man. "Then I'll have a Coors Light for myself and a lawyer for my 'gator."

WISCONSIN

'STAY JUST A LITTLE BIT LONGER'

State Capital: Madison.
Became a State: 29 May 1848.

- ✪ In Wisconsin only one person may take a bath in a tub at one time.

- ✪ Cheese making requires a cheese maker's licence; and Limburger cheese making requires a master cheese maker's licence.

- ✪ It is unlawful to cut a woman's hair.

- ✪ Don't kiss on a train: it's against the law.

- ✪ Whenever two trains meet at an intersection of said tracks, neither shall proceed until the other has passed.

- ✪ In St. Croix women are not allowed to wear anything red in public.

COURTROOM BLUNDERS

The Court addressing a Jury:
Now, as we begin, I must ask you to banish
all present information and prejudice
from your minds, if you have any.

Lawyer: Doctor, how many autopsies
have you performed on dead people?
Witness: All my autopsies have been
performed on dead people.

Lawyer: Please state the nature of
your relationship to the minor child.
Witness: I'm his mother.
Lawyer: And you have been so all of his life?

WYOMING

'LIKE NO PLACE ON EARTH'
State Capital: Cheyenne.
Became a State: 10 July 1890.

✪ It is forbidden to wear a hat that
obstructs people's view in a public
theatre or place of amusement.

*Judge - A law student who marks
his own examination papers.*
H.L. Hencken

COURTROOM BLUNDERS

Lawyer: Did you blow your horn or anything?
Witness: After the accident?
Lawyer: Before the accident.
Witness: Sure, I played for ten years.
I even went to college for it.

Lawyer: Are you qualified to
give a urine sample?
Witness: Yes, I have been
since early childhood.

AUSTRALIA

*When two dogs fight for a bone, and the third
runs off with it, there's a lawyer among the dogs.*
German Proverb

○ Only licensed electricians may
  change a light bulb. Non-electricians
  may be fined for doing this.

○ It is illegal to wear pink hot pants
  after midday on a Sunday.

○ You must have a neck to knee swimsuit
  in order to swim at Brighton Beach.

○ Children may not purchase cigarettes.
  [If they want to smoke them, well

that's a different matter entirely.]

✪ It is against the law to roam the streets wearing black clothes, felt shoes and black shoe polish on your face as these items are a cat burglar's tools.

✪ It is unlawful to walk on the right-hand side of a footpath.

✪ Bar owners are required to stable, water and feed the horses of their patrons.

What's the difference between a mosquito and a lawyer?
One is a blood-sucking parasite, the other is an insect.

How are an apple and a lawyer alike?
They both look good hanging from a tree.

CANADA

There are more lawyers in just Washington, D.C. than in all of Japan. They've got about as many lawyers as we have sumo-wrestlers.
Lee Iococca

- ✪ **35% of a radio station's airtime must be filled with Canadian content.**
- ✪ **You may not pay for a 50c item with pennies only.**
- ✪ **Citizens may not publicly remove bandages.**
- ✪ **It is illegal to kill a sick person by frightening them.**

- ✪ It is against the law to pretend to practise witchcraft.
- ✪ Comic books which depict any illegal acts are banned.
- ✪ Businesses are duty-bound to provide rails for tying up horses.
- ✪ Wooden logs may not be painted.
- ✪ If you are released from prison, it is required that you are given a handgun with bullets and a horse, so you can ride out of town.
- ✪ In Quebec margarine producers can't make their margarine yellow.
- ✪ In Outremont DIY enthusiasts beware: not only do all exterior painting jobs require a permit (for colour) but also, for instance, the City went to the Appeals Court over the exact type of division inside a window frame.

- ✪ The city of Guelph is classified as a no-pee zone.

- ✪ It's illegal to climb trees in Oshawa.

- ✪ It is unlawful to eat ice cream on Bank Street, Ottawa, on a Sunday.

- ✪ You can't drag a dead horse down Yonge Street, Toronto, on a Sunday.

- ✪ It is unlawful to show public affection on a Sunday in Wawa.

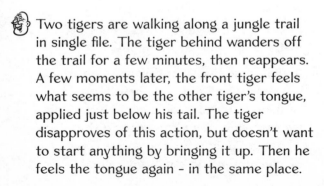 Two tigers are walking along a jungle trail in single file. The tiger behind wanders off the trail for a few minutes, then reappears. A few moments later, the front tiger feels what seems to be the other tiger's tongue, applied just below his tail. The tiger disapproves of this action, but doesn't want to start anything by bringing it up. Then he feels the tongue again - in the same place.

He decides to confront the other tiger and asks him, "Did you just lick me twice in the backside?" The other tiger replies, "Yeah, sorry about that. I just ate a lawyer and I can't get the taste out of my mouth."

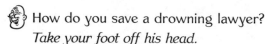 How do you save a drowning lawyer?
Take your foot off his head.

What's the difference between a lawyer and a catfish?
One is a slimy, bottom dwelling, scum sucker. The other is a fish.

What happened to the lawyer who was thrown out of a saloon?
He was disbarred.

DENMARK

*Of course people are getting smarter
nowadays; they are letting lawyers instead
of their conscience be their guides.*
Will Rogers

✪ When driving, you must have
someone in front of your car with a
flag to warn horse-drawn carriages
that a motorcar is coming.

✪ If a horse-drawn carriage is trying to
pass your car and the horse becomes
uneasy, you are required to pull over
and if necessary, cover your car.

○ To try and escape from prison is not illegal. But if you are caught, you must to serve out the remainder of your sentence.

○ You are forbidden to start a car while someone is underneath it.

○ There is a penalty of 20kr for not reporting it when a person has died.

○ You may not be charged for food at an inn unless you are, by your own opinion, 'full'.

○ Restaurants may not charge for water unless it is accompanied by another item such as ice or a slice of lemon.

FRANCE

It is always the best policy to tell the truth, unless, of course, you are an exceptionally good liar.
Jerome K. Jerome

○ Between the hours of 8am and 8pm 70% of music on the radio must be by French artists.

○ It is against the law to kiss on railways in France.

○ No pig owner may call his animal Napoleon.

○ In Antibes it is unlawful to take photos of police officers or police vehicles, even if they are in the background.

✪ In Le Lavandou it is forbidden for you to die on the territory of the commune if you don't have a cemetery plot.

✪ In Paris an ashtray is considered to be a deadly weapon.

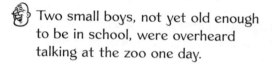 Two small boys, not yet old enough to be in school, were overheard talking at the zoo one day.

"My name is Billy. What's yours?" asked the first boy.

"Tommy," replied the second.

"My Daddy's an accountant. What does your Daddy do for a living?" asked Billy.

Tommy replied, "My Daddy's a lawyer."

"Honest?" asked Billy.

"No, just the regular kind," replied Tommy.

GERMANY

*I was never ruined but twice: once when I
lost a lawsuit, and once when I won one.*
Voltaire

✪ Every office must have a view
of the sky, however small.

✪ A pillow can be considered
a 'passive' weapon.

✪ It is illegal for you to run out of
petrol on the Autobahn.

✪ It is unlawful to wear a mask.

ITALY

- ✪ It is illegal to practise the profession of charlantry.

- ✪ A man may be arrested for wearing a skirt.

- ✪ Striking someone with a fist is considered a felony.

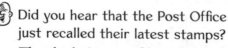 Did you hear that the Post Office just recalled their latest stamps?

They had pictures of lawyers on them ... people kept spitting on the wrong side.

SINGAPORE

Lawyers should never marry other lawyers.
This is called 'inbreeding', from which
comes idiot children and more lawyers.
Kip Lurie

○ The sale of gum is prohibited.

○ Homosexuals are not allowed
to live in the country.

○ Oral sex is illegal unless it is
used as a form of foreplay.

○ Pornography is illegal.

○ You may not walk around your home
nude as it is considered pornographic.

✪ Failure to flush a public toilet after use may result in very hefty fines.

✪ It is considered an offence to enter the country with cigarettes.

✪ Cigarettes are unlawful at all public places.

✪ If you are convicted of littering three times, you will have to clean the streets on Sundays with a bib on saying, "I am a litterer." This will then be broadcast on the local news.

✪ It is against the law to pee in an elevator.

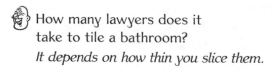 How many lawyers does it take to tile a bathroom?

It depends on how thin you slice them.

SOUTH KOREA

⊙ **Traffic police are required to report all bribes that they receive from motorists.**

*A Lawyer will do anything to win a case,
sometimes he will even tell the truth.*
Patrick Murray

*A lawyer is a learned gentleman who rescues your
estate from you enemies and keeps it to himself.*
Henry Bougham

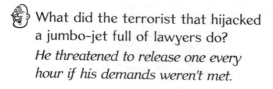 What did the terrorist that hijacked a jumbo-jet full of lawyers do?
He threatened to release one every hour if his demands weren't met.

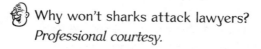 Why won't sharks attack lawyers?
Professional courtesy.

You're trapped in a room with a tiger, a rattlesnake and a lawyer. You have a gun with two bullets. What should you do?
Shoot the lawyer. Twice. To make sure.

SWEDEN

America has a legal system that is the laughing stock in the civilized world.
John Stossel

- ✪ A prince or princess who marries without the consent of the government forfeits the right of succession for his/her children and all other descendants.
- ✪ Prostitution is legal... but it is illegal to use the services of a prostitute.
- ✪ It is against the law to repaint a house without a painting licence and the government's permission.

SWITZERLAND

*The only thing a lawyer won't question
is the legitimacy of his mother.*
W.C. Fields

✪ Clothes may not be hung to dry on a Sunday.

✪ You may not wash your car on a Sunday.

✪ It is considered an offence to mow
your lawn on a Sunday, because
it causes too much noise.

✪ It is illegal to flush the toilet after
10pm if you live in an apartment.

✪ After 10pm a man may not relieve
himself while standing up.

○ Though it is unlawful to produce, store, sell and trade absinth (special alcohol), it is legal to consume it.

○ You will be punished if you forget that your car keys are inside the car and you leave the car open.

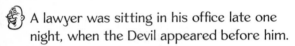 A lawyer was sitting in his office late one night, when the Devil appeared before him.

The Devil said, "I have a proposition for you. You can win every case you try, for the rest of your life. Your clients will adore you, your colleagues will stand in awe of you, and you will make obscene amounts of money. All I want in exchange is your soul, your wife's soul, your children's souls, the souls of your parents, grandparents, and parents-in-law, and the souls of all of your friends and law partners."

The lawyer thought about this for a moment, then asked, "So, what's the catch?"

THAILAND

- ⚙ You must not leave your house if you have no underwear on.
- ⚙ You must wear a shirt while driving a car.
- ⚙ You may not step on any of the nation's currency.

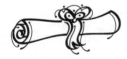

The one great principle of English law
is to make business for itself.
Charles Dickens

One afternoon, a wealthy lawyer was riding in the back of his limousine when he saw two men eating grass by the side of the road. He ordered his driver to stop and he got out to investigate.

"Why are you eating grass?" he asked one man.

"We don't have any money for food," the poor man replied.

"Well come along with me then."

"But sir, I have a wife with two children."

"Bring them along! And you, come with us too!" he said to the other man.

"But sir, I have a wife with six children!" the second man answered.

"Well bring them too."

They all climbed into the car, which
was no easy task, even for a limo.

Once underway, one of the poor fellows
said, "Sir, you are too kind. Thank
you for taking all of us with you."

The lawyer replied, "No problem, the
grass at my home is about two feet tall."

 An airplane was having engine trouble,
and the pilot instructed the cabin
crew to prepare the passengers
for an emergency landing.

A few minutes later, the pilot asked
the flight attendants if everyone
was buckled in and ready.

"All set back here, Captain," came the
reply, "except the lawyers are still going
around passing out business cards."

UNITED KINGDOM

*There are three sorts of lawyers
- able, unable and lamentable.*
Robert Smith Surtees

✪ You may not fish for salmon on Sundays.

✪ It is against the law to be a drunk
in possession of a cow.

✪ If someone knocks on your door
and requires the use of your toilet,
you must let them enter.

✪ All English males over the age
14 are to carry out two or so
hours of longbow practice a week

supervised by the local clergy.

○ London Hackney Carriages
(taxis/cabs) must carry a bale
of hay and a sack of oats.

○ The severest penalties will be suffered
by any commoner who doth permit his
animal to have carnal knowledge of a pet
of the Royal House [enacted by George I].

○ It is unlawful to be drunk on licensed
premises [i.e. in a pub or bar].

○ It is illegal for two adult men to have sex
in the same house as a third person.

○ If you come across a washed-up dead
whale do not take the tail, as it has
to be given to the queen. [This law
was passed in the 14th century to
ensure the queen had a good supply
of whalebone for dressmaking and
in order to keep her figure trim.]

- ✪ Any person found breaking a boiled egg at the narrow end would be sentenced to 24 hours in the village stocks [enacted by Edward VI].

- ✪ It is unlawful to stand within one hundred yards of the reigning monarch when not wearing socks [enacted by Edward VI].

- ✪ Chelsea pensioners may not be impersonated. [Until 1965 - when the death penalty was abolished - it was a hanging offence to impersonate a Chelsea pensioner. Do it now and you will be charged with fraud. This is because of many free valuable handouts the pensioners attract. Watch the tennis at Wimbledon every year where you will see the lads enjoying themselves gratis.]

- ✪ A bed may not be hung out of a window.

- ✪ It is illegal for a lady to eat chocolates on a public conveyance.

- Any boy under the age of ten may not see a naked mannequin.

- It is unlawful for a Member of Parliament to enter the House of Commons wearing a full suit of armour. [This dates back to 1313 and this ban is still in force.]

- Destroying or defacing money is illegal.

- All steam locomotives are limited to 4 mph on roads.

- If a steam locomotive is driven on roads, a man must walk in front of the vehicle with a red flag during the day and a red lantern at night to warn passers-by.

- Committing suicide is classified as a capital crime.

- Interfering with the mail or sleeping with the consort of the queen is classed as treason, and as such, carries a maximum penalty of death.

- ✪ Placing a postage stamp that bears the queen (or king) upside down is considered treason.

- ✪ A licence is required to keep a lunatic.

- ✪ Damaging the grass is illegal.

- ✪ In Chester, you can only shoot a Welsh person with a bow and arrow inside the city walls and after midnight.

- ✪ In Hereford, you may not shoot a Welsh person on a Sunday with a longbow in the Cathedral Close.

- ✪ In Liverpool, it is illegal for a woman to be topless in public except as a clerk in a tropical fish store.

- ✪ In York, it is perfectly legal to shoot a Scotsman with a bow and arrow, apart from on Sundays.

Lawyers are like rhinoceroses: thick skinned, shortsighted, and always ready to charge.
David Mellor

A man who never graduated from school might steal from a freight car. But a man who attends college and graduates as a lawyer might steal the whole railroad.
Theodore Roosevelt

Make crime pay.
Become a lawyer.
Will Rogers

How many contract lawyers does it take to change a light bulb?

WHEREAS, the party of the first part, also known as "Lawyer", and the party of the second part, also known as "Light Bulb", do hereby and forthwith agree to a transaction wherein the party of the second part (Light Bulb) shall be removed from the current position as a result of failure to perform previously agreed upon duties, i.e. the lighting, elucidation, and otherwise illumination of the area ranging from the front (North) door, through the entryway, terminating at an area just inside the primary living area, demarcated by the beginning of the carpet, any spill over illumination being at the option of the party of the second part (Light Bulb) and not required by the aforementioned agreement between the parties. The aforementioned removal transaction shall include, but not.....................!!!!!!

Also available

ISBN 1-905102-02-X – £3.99

Also available

ISBN 1-905102-16-X – £4.99

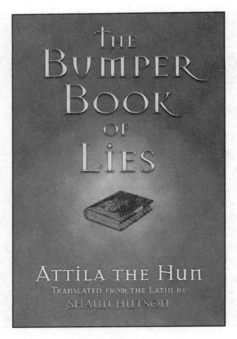

THE BUMPER BOOK OF LIES

ATTILA THE HUN

TRANSLATED FROM THE LATIN BY

SHAUN HUTSON

Also available

ISBN 1-905102-37-2 – £8.99

Also available

ISBN 1-905102-23-2 – £2.99

the little eBay book

UNOFFICIAL   UNOFFICIAL

The website's most weird and wondrous...

Also available

ISBN 1-905102-19-4 – £2.99

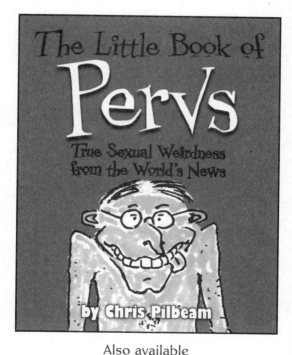

Also available

ISBN 1-905102-38-0 – £2.99

All Crombie Jardine books are available
from your High Street bookshops, Amazon,
Littlehampton Book Services, or Bookpost
(P.O.Box 29, Douglas,
Isle of Man, IM99 1BQ.
tel: 01624 677 237, email: bookshop@enterprise.
net. Free postage and packing within the UK).